# The
# Margaret Tarrant
# Nursery Rhyme
# Book

# The Margaret Tarrant Nursery Rhyme Book

Collins

William Collins Sons & Co Ltd
London · Glasgow · Sydney · Auckland
Toronto · Johannesburg


First published 1944
Revised edition 1985
© illustrations William Collins Sons & Co Ltd 1944

British Library Cataloguing in Publication Data

Tarrant, Margaret
    The Margaret Tarrant nursery rhyme book.
    1. Nursery rhymes, English
    I. Title
    398'.8    PZ8.3

    ISBN 0-00-183732-X

Printed in Hong Kong by South China Printing Co.

# Contents

## Jack and Jill

Jack and Jill
    went up the hill
To fetch a pail
    of water;
Jack fell down and
    broke his crown,
And Jill came
    tumbling after.

# See-Saw
# Margery Daw

See-saw, Margery Daw,
    Johnny shall have a new master;
He shall have but a penny a day
    Because he can't work any faster.

# To Market – To Market

To market, to market,
    To buy a fat pig;
Home again, home again,
    Jiggety jig.

To market, to market,
    To buy a fat hog;
Home again, home again,
    Jiggety jog.

This little pig
went to market.

This little pig stayed at home;

This little pig had roast beef

This little pig
had none;

This little pig cried
"Wee wee, wee, wee!"
All the way home.

# There was an Old Woman
# who lived in a Shoe

There was an old woman
    Who lived in a shoe;
She had so many children
    She didn't know what to do;

She gave them some broth
    Without any bread,
She whipped them all soundly,
    And sent them to bed.

# Pussy Cat —
# Pussy Cat

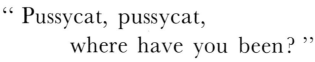

" Pussycat, pussycat,
    where have you been? "
" I've been to London,
    to visit the Queen."

" Pussycat, pussycat,
    what did you there? "
" I frightened a little mouse
    under her chair."

# Hickery
# Dickery
# Dock!

Hickery, Dickery, Dock!
The mouse ran up the clock,
The clock struck one,
The mouse ran down,
Hickery, Dickery, Dock.

# Little Jack Horner

Little Jack Horner
Sat in a corner,
Eating his Christmas pie;
He put in his thumb
And pulled out a plum —
Saying, " Oh what a
good boy am I ! "

Little Miss Muffet,
Sat on a tuffet,
Eating her curds
and whey;

There came a great spider,
And sat down
beside her,

And frightened
Miss Muffet
away!

Margaret W. Tarrant

# Little Boy Blue

Little Boy Blue, come
    Blow up your horn,
The sheep's in the meadow,
    The cow's in the corn.

Where is the boy who
    Looks after the sheep?
Under the haystack,
    Fast asleep.

# Little Bo-Peep

Little Bo-Peep, she lost her sheep,
And didn't know where to find them,
Leave them alone and they'll come home,
And carry their tails behind them.

Then up she took her little crook,
Determined for to find them;
She found them indeed, but it made her
heart bleed,
For they'd left their tails behind them.

It happened one day, as Bo-Peep did stray,
Into a meadow hard by,
There she espied their tails side by side,
All hung on a tree to dry.

She heaved a sigh and wiped her eye,
Then went o'er hill and dale,
And tried what she could as a shepherdess should,
To tack each sheep to its tail.

# Sing a Song of Sixpence

Sing a song of sixpence,
　　A pocket full of rye;
Four and twenty blackbirds,
　　Baked in a pie.

When the pie was opened,
　　The birds began to sing,
Wasn't that a dainty dish
　　To set before the king?

The king was in the counting-house,
　　Counting out his money;
The queen was in her parlour
　　Eating bread and honey.

The maid was in the garden,
　　Hanging out some clothes,
When down came a blackbird,
　　And pecked off her nose.

*NOTE: But down came little Jenny Wren and popped it on again.*

# Oh dear, what can the matter be?

Oh dear, what can the matter be?
Oh dear, what can the matter be?
Oh dear, what can the matter be?
    Johnnie's so long at the fair.

He promised to buy me
    a bunch of blue ribbons,
He promised to buy me
    a bunch of blue ribbons,
He promised to buy me
    a bunch of blue ribbons,
To tie up my bonnie brown hair.

He promised to bring me
    a basket of posies,
A garland of lilies,
    a garland of roses,
A little straw hat to set off
    the blue ribbons,
That tie up my bonnie brown hair.

# Mary, Mary,
# quite Contrary

" Mary, Mary, quite contrary,
    How does your garden grow? "
" With silver bells, and cockle shells
    And pretty maids all in a row."

# The Queen of Hearts

The Queen of Hearts
She made some tarts,
All on a summer's day;

The Knave of Hearts,
He stole the tarts,
And took them clean away.

The King of Hearts
Called for the tarts,
And beat the Knave full sore;

The Knave of Hearts
Brought back the tarts,
And vowed he'd steal no more.

# Ride a Cock-horse
# to Banbury Cross

Ride a Cock-horse,
To Banbury Cross
To see a fine lady
Ride on a white horse.

Rings on her fingers
And bells on her toes,
She shall have music
Wherever she goes.

Hey diddle diddle

The cat and     the fiddle

The cow jumped     over the moon,

The little dog laughed to see such sport.     And the dish ran away with the spoon

Margaret W. Tarrant

# Simple Simon

Simple Simon met a pieman,
    Going to the fair;
Says Simple Simon to the pieman,
    " Let me taste your ware."

Says the pieman to Simple Simon,
    " Show me first your penny."
Says Simple Simon to the pieman,
    " Indeed I have not any."

Simple Simon went to look
    If plums grew on a thistle;
He pricked his fingers very much,
    Which made poor Simon whistle.

Simple Simon went a-fishing
    For to catch a whale;
All the water he could find
    Was in his mother's pail:

He went to catch a dicky bird,
    And thought he could not fail,
Because he had a little salt
    To put upon its tail.

He went for water with a sieve,
    But soon it ran all through;
And now poor Simple Simon
    Bids you all adieu.

# Rock-a-bye Baby

Rock-a-bye baby,
　　On the tree top,
When the wind blows,
　　The cradle will rock.

When the bough breaks,
　　The cradle will fall,
Down will come baby,
　　Cradle and all.

# Index of first lines